T0131282

Spiritual Biographies
FOR YOUNG READERS

Thich Nhat Hanh
Buddhism in Action

Maura D. Shaw • Illustrations by Stephen Marchesi

With the assistance of the Green Mountain Dharma Center

Walking Together, Finding the Way
SKYLIGHT PATHS Publishing
Woodstock, Vermont

Who Is Thich Nhat Hanh?

Thich Nhat Hanh is a Buddhist monk from a faraway country called Vietnam, but he now lives in France. His name sounds like "tick not haan." But you might like to call him Thây ("tay"), which means "teacher." That's what all the children who visit Thây with their families call him.

People come from around the world to learn from Thây about how to be more mindful, and how to live in peace and happiness on our beautiful Earth.

When you learn about Thich Nhat Hanh's life, you will see what makes him amazing. He shows people how to love each other and to not be violent. He loves to walk and talk with children and their families.

A Poem by Thich Nhat Hanh

Thây wrote this short poem.

Kiss the Earth

Walk and touch peace every moment.
Walk and touch happiness every moment.
Each step brings a fresh breeze.
Each step makes a flower bloom.
Kiss the Earth with your feet.
Bring the Earth your love and happiness.
The Earth will be safe
when we feel safe in ourselves.

Thây leads a walk for peace.

Thây's Life in and beyond Vietnam

Thich Nhat Hanh loved his homeland of Vietnam, where the air was warm and gentle and rice paddies covered the green wetlands. He also loved to follow the peaceful way of living that the Buddha, another great teacher, taught many years ago. When he was sixteen Thây became a Buddhist monk.

Statues of the Buddha show his calm face.

When there was a war in his country, Thây tried bravely to stop the fighting. Instead, the government made him leave the country he loved. Since then, he has spent his life bringing the teachings of the Buddha to the whole world.

Thây was only a teenager when he became a monk.

7

The big bell at Plum Village calls everyone for meals and meditation.

Founding Plum Village

When the war in Vietnam finally ended, Thây still could not go home. He and his friends bought an old farm in France, which they named Plum Village, and they fixed up the buildings and planted gardens and plum trees. People who had escaped from Vietnam came to live and work at Plum Village, where they could feel safe and learn to be happy and peaceful again. They grew their favorite special vegetables from Vietnam so they would feel at home.

Welcomed by Daffodils

One day in the early spring, Thây and his friends at Plum Village were surprised to see a whole hillside of bright yellow daffodils blooming. Thousands and thousands of flowers opened their buds and waved at Thây and the other Buddhist monks and nuns. Thây was amazed at the beauty of these splendid flowers and so each year he holds a Daffodil Festival on the first Sunday in March. People come to listen to Thây's teachings, walk on the hillside among the flowers, and enjoy tea, meditation, songs, and dancing.

A young girl plays her violin among the flowers.

Thây teaches the young monks from Vietnam.

Life in Plum Village

Plum Village is Thây's home now, and thousands of people still come from all over the world to learn from him. Many families come to this beautiful place in the country for their summer vacation. They want to spend time with Thây and learn about the important work that he is doing.

Thây believes that each person—big or small—has the chance to make the world a better place to live.

Now It's Your Turn
A MEDITATION TIME OUT

Have you ever had a "time out," when someone asked you to sit for a moment and think about something that just happened? After this quiet time, you probably felt a little better than you did before.

Have you ever just sat outside and thought about the grass, the clouds, the wind, and the birds? When you do take a little time to sit quietly, how does it make you feel? Try this: Sit still and be quiet and close your eyes. Take a long, deep breath. After a few minutes, open your eyes and smile.

You can try Thây's walking meditation, too—but keep your eyes open when you're walking! Practice smiling while you walk. Thây teaches that smiling is good for you. He tries to smile as often as he can.

Sharing Peace

During the first ten minutes of each day's teaching time at Plum Village, Thây talks to the children before they go out

to play in the fresh air. He talks about the need for people to be mindful in their everyday lives, which means that we should be aware of what we are doing and concentrate on enjoying it before we do something else.

When we are mindful we are peaceful, and when we are peaceful it helps other people to be peaceful, too.

Letting Go of Anger

Thây also talks about how to let go of anger. You can think of anger as being like a friend who is pulling on your arm when you wish he or she would let go. Doesn't it feel good when your friend lets go of your arm and you are free?

You can practice letting go of your angry feelings. When you feel angry, breathe in to feel calm, and then breathe out, imagining that your anger is going out with your breath.

If you have peace in your heart and a smile on your lips, you can be like a flower. Breathing in, you feel calm. You are fresh as a flower. Breathing out, you are not going to get angry. You are solid as a mountain.

Thây says, "Make good use of the flower and the mountain in you and you will not be affected by what other people say and what they do to you. If you begin to practice at a young age, you will be able to help so many people."

Life at Plum Village

Buddhist monks and nuns and other friends study and live with Thây. They do many of the things that other people do each day, but they also spend a lot of time praying, meditating, and practicing mindfulness.

Because Buddhists believe in caring for all life and don't want to harm any animals, they decide not to eat meat. A lot of the food at Thây's home is grown in their gardens. Even the slugs who want to eat the plants in the greenhouses are cared for—every evening in the springtime, Thây's students pick the slugs off the leaves, put them gently in pails, and carry them out to the forest, where they can eat all the leaves they want!

Mindfulness is paying attention to what is around you, in the present moment, without worrying about the past or the future.

Slugs in the gardens at Plum Village are carried to the forest and set free.

22

An Amazing Life

Thich Nhat Hanh began his work as a simple teenage Buddhist monk in Vietnam, and through his deep belief in peace and mindfulness, he has become a teacher for the world. Isn't that amazing?

Thay's Poem about Peace

Thây wrote this poem, too. Have you ever tried to write poems?

Peace Is Every Step

Peace is every step.

The shining red sun is my heart.

Each flower smiles with me.

How green, how fresh all that grows.

How cool the wind blows.

Peace is every step.

It turns the endless path to joy.

Now It's Your Turn
GROWING SEEDS

The next time you see a colorful package of seeds for planting, think about the seeds inside. How can seeds be used to help people? A package of seeds might cost fifty cents or one dollar. If you plant them and take care of them, would you have more than one dollar's worth of food?

Thây says that inside of us are the beginnings of feelings, beginnings that are much like the seeds that we plant in the ground. Some of these "seeds," such as anger or self-ishness, we do not want to grow. We shouldn't water them

26

by fighting or by acting mean. Other seeds, such as joy and wanting to help others, we do want to grow. We water those good seeds so that they will grow big inside of us. And by sharing and being kind, we can help water the good seeds in our friends, too.

Now It's Your Turn

HOW WOULD YOU MAKE A CHANGE?

Make up a sentence or a poem telling about something that you think is wrong and that you would like to change. Tell about how you could try to make this happen.

You might like to draw a picture of the world as you hope it will be.

Fascinating Fact

Plum Village is named for its 1,250 plum trees, which are cared for by the people from Vietnam—and many other places around the world—who now make their home at Thây's retreat center. The money earned from the sale of the plum crop is sent to Vietnam to buy medicine and to pay for daycare centers and schools for poor children.

Important Events
in the Life of Thich Nhat Hanh

1942—Thich Nhat Hanh became a Buddhist monk at the age of sixteen.

1950—He founded a center for Buddhist studies in South Vietnam.

1961—He came to the United States to study and to teach.

1963—Thich Nhat Hanh returned to Vietnam to lead nonviolent protests against the war.

1964—Exiled from both North and South Vietnam for his antiwar activities, he began his mission to spread Buddhist teachings and a message of mindfulness.

1967—He was nominated for the Nobel Peace Prize by Martin Luther King Jr.

1968—Thich Nhat Hanh led the Vietnamese Buddhist group to the Paris peace talks to help end the war in Vietnam.

1982—He founded Plum Village in France, a retreat center and Buddhist community.

1980s-2000s—Thich Nhat Hanh published more than seventy-five books, including books of poetry, spiritual teaching, and meditation, and he taught workshops around the world.

Important Words to Know

Buddhism One of the world's major religions, founded in India by Siddhartha Gautama, known as the Buddha, nearly 2,500 years ago.

Dharma The way, or law, of living as a Buddhist.

Meditation The practice of quieting your mind to become peaceful and calm, sometimes done by sitting still and sometimes by mindful walking.

Mindfulness Paying attention to what is around you, in the present moment, without worrying about the past or the future.

Monks and nuns Men and women who decide to spend their lives in prayer, meditation, and service to others. They do not marry and may live in communities or small groups. Monks and nuns are found in Buddhist, Hindu, and Christian faiths.

Thây Word that means "honored teacher" in Vietnamese.

Thich Nhat Hanh: Buddhism in Action

2004 First Printing
Text © 2004 by SkyLight Paths Publishing
Illustrations © 2002 by Stephen Marchesi

All rights reserved. No part of this book may be reproduced or transmitted in any form or by any means, electronic or mechanical, including photocopying, recording, or by any information storage and retrieval system, without permission in writing from the publisher.

For information regarding permission to reprint material from this book, please mail or fax your request in writing to SkyLight Paths Publishing, Permissions Department, at the address / fax number listed below, or e-mail your request to permissions@skylightpaths.com.

Library of Congress Cataloging-in-Publication Data
Shaw, Maura D.
Thich Nhat Hanh : Buddhism in action / Maura D. Shaw ; illustrations by Stephen Marchesi.
        p. cm. — (Spiritual biographies for young readers)
Summary: A biography of Buddhist monk Thich Nhat Hanh which emphasizes the spiritual beliefs that guided him in trying to prevent war in Vietnam and in striving to make the world a better place in which to live. Includes activities and a note for parents and teachers.
ISBN 1-893361-87-X
1. Nhat Hanh, Thich—Juvenile literature. 2. Buddhism—Social aspects—Juvenile literature. 3. Religious leaders—Biography—Juvenile literature. 4. Spiritual life—Buddhism—Juvenile literature. [1. Nhat Hanh, Thich. 2. Buddhist monks. 3. Buddhism. 4. Spiritual life—Buddhism.] I. Marchesi, Stephen, ill. II. Title. III. Series.
BQ962.H36 S53 2003
294.3'927'092—dc22
                                                                                        2003011867

10 9 8 7 6 5 4 3 2 1
Manufactured in Hong Kong

A special thank you to Shelly Angers for her help in creating the activities in this book.

Grateful acknowledgment is given for permission to reprint material from the following sources: photos on pages 5, 7, and 15 © Green Mountain Dharma Center; photos on pages 6, 8, 16, 25, and 31 © Simon Chaput; photos on pages 11, 17, and 30 by Trân Van Minh, courtesy of Parallax Press, Berkeley, California, www.parallax.org; photos/artwork on pages 18, 28, and 29 courtesy of *The Mindfulness Bell,* published by the Community of Mindful Living; photo on page 13 © Gaetano Maida.

Poems on pages 4 and 24 are reprinted from *The Long Road Turns to Joy: A Guide to Walking Meditation* (1996) by Thich Nhat Hanh with permission of Parallax Press, Berkeley, California, www.parallax.org.

Some images © Clipart.com

Every effort has been made to trace and acknowledge copyright holders of all material used in this book. The publisher apologizes for any errors or omissions that may remain, and asks that any omissions be brought to their attention so they may be corrected in future editions.

SkyLight Paths, "Walking Together, Finding the Way" and colophon are trademarks of LongHill Partners, Inc., registered in the U.S. Patent and Trademark Office.

Walking Together, Finding the Way
Published by SkyLight Paths Publishing
A Division of LongHill Partners, Inc.
Sunset Farm Offices, Route 4, P.O. Box 237
Woodstock, VT 05091
Tel: (802) 457-4000   Fax: (802) 457-4004
www.skylightpaths.com